Investing 101:

A Basic Guide to Investing for Beginners

By

Kirk G. Meyer

Investing 101: A Basic Guide to Investing for Beginners
by Kirk G. Meyer

Investing 101:

A Basic Guide to Investing for Beginners

Copyright © 2016 by Kirk G. Meyer

All rights reserved. This includes the right to reproduce any portion of this book in any form.

Disclaimer: Every effort was made to describe the information in this book in an accurate manner as of the publication date. The author makes no guarantees regarding the information in this book.

Investing 101: A Basic Guide to Investing for Beginners
by Kirk G. Meyer

Why You Should Buy this Book

Why should you buy any book? You are looking for either entertainment or education, a lot of people turn to books for these two purposes. Well, I hope that this book is both entertaining in the manner that it will educate you on investments. Everyone needs to take an active role in their investments as the government is reducing its role in people's retirement. Therefore, it is up to you to understand what you need to do in order to stay on top of your investments mainly for retirement purposes. Let us face it; no one will be helping us in our retirement years other than ourselves.

This book touches on the basics of a subject that can be as complex as you want it to be or as basic as you want. That choice is up to you, and only you know where your comfort level is when it comes to your investments. But this book will give anyone the basic knowledge that they would need to manage and to a degree excel at managing their own investment portfolio.

As a person who has three advanced degrees, one being in Financial Planning, I am here to tell you that with a little work on your part a financial planner is not always needed. This book will assist you so that you can manage your investment portfolio for yourself without the assistance of someone who will be charging you what could be a hefty fee.

Investing 101: A Basic Guide to Investing for Beginners by Kirk G. Meyer

Why I Wrote this Book

I wrote this book to assist and help others in the area of investments. As I stated earlier, it can complex, or it can be simple in nature. The choice of which is up to you. But in this book, we will take a simple approach to investments and try to make them understandable for everyone, not just those with advanced degrees or professional licenses. I have always taken the approach of making anything complex in nature and reducing it to its simplest form. I have done this in my education as well as my professional life. While not always easy to do or achievable it is something that makes things easier for me to understand and comprehend.

Investing does not need to be difficult and in many instances, simple is actually better as we will look at later. What makes me qualified to write such a book you may ask? I have over 15 years of experience in financial areas with the Federal government covering a wide range of topics. And as far as my education I hold a Master's of Financial Planning, a Master's in Accounting and an MBA. I am educated in the formal sense as well as having read countless books on finance and financial matters. All of this has allowed me to form a unique approach to investments that I think anyone can and will understand.

At the end of the book, I will explain how you will be able to gain access to my email newsletter and receive some free valuable gifts made available to those who purchase my books.

Investing 101: A Basic Guide to Investing for Beginners by Kirk G. Meyer

Table of Contents

Why You Should Buy this Book 3

Why I Wrote this Book 4

Table of Contents 5

Introduction 6

Primary Investments 10

Where to Invest and How 13

The Impact of Taxes 17

Investment Plans 23

Returns and How to Consider Them 28

Different Asset Classes 33

Diversification 39

General Thoughts 43

Conclusion 47

Thank You for Your Purchase 49

About Kirk G. Meyer 50

How to Contact Kirk G. Meyer 51

   One Last Chance for the Free Gifts! 51

Other Books by Kirk G. Meyer 52

Investing 101: A Basic Guide to Investing for Beginners by Kirk G. Meyer

Introduction

What is an investment? Many people think of stocks when they think of investments. While that is indeed true, it is far from the complete picture. Investments can range from something that someone may consider of little value, like corn to a farmer who plans on storing it for use later. Gold and silver bought as supposed hedges against inflation to rental property that someone buys and manages to produce a monthly income stream. And the purchase of bonds to provide a stream of interest payments going into the future. As you can see, investments can take on the form of many different things and not just stocks or equities. It is anything that has value and can be exchanged for something else of value at a future point in time.

A wise person who wants to maximize their investment return and minimize risk will look at a wide variety of investments to own and include in their portfolio. We will examine the what and how to do this in a non-complex nature and try to ensure that anyone can manage their own portfolio. It does not take anything special to do this just will and a basic understanding of how the individual investments work. Something you will be able to do by the end of the book.

But even after reading this book and maybe others some people will still not feel comfortable in managing their own portfolios. For those people I suggest a good fee-only planner to help guide you on your way to establishing a financial plan and may be monitoring your progress. I do not see the need to pay someone on a

Investing 101: A Basic Guide to Investing for Beginners
by Kirk G. Meyer

continuous basis when a fee-only planner can achieve the same results and leave more of your money where it belongs, your investment portfolio.

So how do you start and maximize your investments? Well to begin with you need to diversify your holdings, keep your expenses as low as possible, have a well-developed financial plan to follow, save and invest early in your career and as often as you can. The more you save early, the better off you will be in the long run as money compounds over time and can work for you in ways you most likely never imagined.

But do you have to take an active role in your investments? The answer here is a resounding no you do not. In most every instance I know of a passive approach is almost always more lucrative than that of one that is actively managed. Even the great investor Warren Buffett who has outperformed the S&P 500 most years will tell you as he does almost every year at the annual Berkshire Shareholder's meeting investing in a passive indexed fund will beat most actively managed funds. And to put his money where his mouth is, he has challenged anyone to try to beat an indexed fund for a decade. To date, no one has been able to do this for an entire decade.

So why do people decide to take an active role in their investments you are asking? Well, there is the pride and the feeling that we know better than most and are capable of beating the markets. While that may be the case on a short-term basis, it is nearly impossible over the long haul. Yes, compound interest will aid you in

Investing 101: A Basic Guide to Investing for Beginners
by Kirk G. Meyer

beating the markets it is not the only factor one needs to consider. The other that will eat away at your earnings as fast as the compounding will add are fees and commissions associated with actively managed funds.

Let us look at two people who are just graduating from college with their degrees. Both are entering the workforce at the age of 22. On the one hand, we have Jane who will take a passive approach to her investing, and we have Bill who will take an active role in his investments. Jane had a personal finance course in college and started an Individual Retirement Account and saved the maximum allowed in an indexed exchange traded fund that tracks the entire stock market with an expense rate of 0.2%. Jane also started saving in her IRA immediately at the age of 22 and saved the same amount for 45 years until she was able to retire at age 67, her full retirement age. When Jane retires, she will have amassed $1.581 million in her IRA if you assume a 10% return, 0.2% in fees, no commissions and all taxes deferred with a 3% adjustment for inflation. And yes a 10% return on the stock market is considered average since 1900 with some periods vastly outperforming others and at other times being underproductive in nature.

Now Bill starts investing in his IRA at age 30 so he only will have 37 years to have his funds compounded before he retires. He is also investing in actively managed mutual funds which on average charge 1.3% in fees, pays a financial advisor 1% of assets under management and gets the average return for someone who participates in actively managed portfolios, 4% a year after inflation's

Investing 101: A Basic Guide to Investing for Beginners
by Kirk G. Meyer

adjustment. That is over half of what Jane makes by investing in a passive account. Then when you consider Bill is also paying 2.3% in fees his return for the 37-year period is only 1.7%. That is some difference as his IRA at retirement will only have $285,000. Why does Bill have so much less? One, it is on the fees, and people tend to make costly mistakes when they manage their own funds, earning 6% less than the overall stock market on average. In the same scenario had Bill even started at age 22 and not 30 he would only have $374,000, still a far cry from Jane's account balance.

So how do you know how long an investment will take to double? The simple answer is the "Rule of 72". That is you take your return, in the case above 10% and divide it into 72 for a 7.2 answer or about seven years. So in the event you are earning 10% you can expect your money to double every seven years. But here is where the power of compounding takes over and really kicks into high gear. After fourteen years you have actually increased your investment four-fold, 2x2. And it goes from there so if you invested for 42 years your investment would increase 64 times the initial investment or 2x2x2x2x2x2. That is the real power of compound interest.

Investing 101: A Basic Guide to Investing for Beginners by Kirk G. Meyer

Primary Investments

The most common types of investments as I alluded to earlier are equities or stocks. Bonds are a close second to equities with thousands of people investing in them as well. We will examine both in this sections and define each in a simple manner.

Equities or a single stock simply represents a piece of ownership in a company by whoever own the equity. Equities can be owned by individuals, other companies, mutual funds, and exchange-traded funds. The price someone is willing to pay for equity is based on its intrinsic value. Intrinsic value is basically the future income stream of a company that is projected to be produced and discounted back to its present value to account for the time value of money. There are several ways to calculate the intrinsic value, and all are beyond the scope of this book. But if you want to see what an equity's intrinsic value is, look for an on-line calculator and plug in your assumptions to see what the output is. In stocks, you take on more risks as you can either profit in the company's success, or you may lose money if it fails. That is one of the prices of ownership.

A bond, on the other hand, is a loan to a company or government. It acts like an IOU of sorts between you and whoever you bought the bond from. Bonds are seen as safer investments than equities as in ownership you could lose all you invested in the event of bankruptcy. Bondholders, on the other hand, are paid before shareholders in a bankruptcy proceeding. And when a bond is redeemed it will have paid the bondholder

Investing 101: A Basic Guide to Investing for Beginners
by Kirk G. Meyer

interest for a set period of time and all of the principal upon maturity. But bonds do carry rate sensitivity risk which means you could have a bond pay 5% then rates go up, and bonds start paying 6%. This means your bond will pay less than others resulting in lost earning opportunities causing the price of your bond to go down. Of course, this is irrelevant if you plan on keeping your bonds until they mature.

Now most people are not lucky enough or have enough money to invest in equities and bonds when they are first released to the public. Almost everyone who owns equities and to a large degree bonds have purchased them on the secondary market. That is to say on the New York Stock Exchange or NYSE or NASDAQ. Here are where equities are bought and sold on a daily basis from anyone who wants to sell and purchased by anyone who is wanting to buy. On the secondary market, the price is determined by numerous factors, but the main one is simply supply and demand.

Most people find it difficult to manage large portfolios of equities and different bonds, so the financial world introduced the advent of the mutual fund. This is a collection of equities, bonds, cash or a combination of the three that are sold as a single share. Mutual funds are priced daily at the end of the trading activities by the Net Asset Value or NAV. Mutual funds allow smaller investors the ability to invest in many equities or bonds at a single time through large pools of money that are managed by professionals. In later sections, we will look at exchange traded funds which are relatively new but act in a similar fashion as mutual funds.

Investing 101: A Basic Guide to Investing for Beginners
by Kirk G. Meyer

Equities are the best way to build wealth, but they come at a greater risk as well. That is why most people should invest in mutual funds or exchange-traded funds to diminish their overall risk and exposure to any one company. While the intrinsic value is adequate in aiding us to determine an equities price it is not without its flaws. Equities are extremely volatile in nature due to several factors. Changes in technology, economics, inflation and individual preference can have positive and negative impacts on an equities intrinsic value. And one should and can never discount the human factor when it comes to the prices of equities, fear, and greed. The age of buy and hold is going away despite what Warren Buffett's Berkshire Hathaway does with the majority of its holdings. On average an individual will only hold an investment for an average of fewer than six months.

If one were to use only the intrinsic value and ignore the other outside factors, that person or mutual fund would be holding the equity far longer than six months. This activity creates higher fees for both individuals and mutual funds. And in the case of mutual funds, it creates a taxable event which further eats into one's profits and it could do the same for an individual.

Investing 101: A Basic Guide to Investing for Beginners by Kirk G. Meyer

Where to Invest and How

When it comes to where and how to invest, there are numerous options available you these days. Many years ago you had very few options when it came to buying equities or bonds. You had to go through one of the full-service brokerage firms, such as Goldman Sachs. And let us face it that these firms mainly catered to the high net worth individual or company for their business. And they also charged fairly high fees and commissions to buy and sell equities and bonds for people.

Then with more and more people getting involved with investing in the late 1980's and into the 1990's discount brokers began to appear such as TD Ameritrade. Here people could invest in smaller amounts and for lower fees and commissions. Thus enabling more people to take advantage of the equity markets. The main difference between a full-service brokerage firm and a discount broker was that discount brokers provided less in the way of services and advice to their customers. Enabling them to charge lower fees and commissions.

However, with the advent of the Internet discount brokers have taken on an entirely new role and have opened up the markets to even more people. Even at a discount broker where you have an advisor assisting with your trades, you can spend hundreds of dollars executing a single transaction. With on-line brokers, this can be done for less than $10 a trade. If you buy and sell often, this can make a huge difference in your bottom line in the investment portfolios you manage. Over time these

Investing 101: A Basic Guide to Investing for Beginners by Kirk G. Meyer

fees can cost you tens of thousands of lost income in your portfolio.

And in today's investing environment brokers are not the only option you have. Many financial companies that operate mutual funds and exchange traded funds offer brokerage type services for their own products. In these instances, many of the fees are waived if you invest the minimum that they require. T. Rowe Price and Vanguard are two such companies that offer these services directly to you the investor. And in a few instances, they will even allow the purchase of equities outside of their family of funds for a fee. So do not limit yourself to just brokerage firms but look at financial companies that run mutual funds and exchange traded funds.

Fees in mutual funds can vary greatly. In an average actively managed fund you can expect to pay about 1.3% a year in management fees. This compares to about .2% a year in a passively managed mutual fund. Now that may not seem like a lot to you now but a spread of 1.1% over a 30-year period could cost you tens of thousands of dollars in your portfolio. And that is not all, in some mutual funds, there is a fee or load to buy or sell that can be as high as 5% of the purchase price. I cannot stress this enough, never pay a load to buy a mutual fund as that generally is nothing more than a sales cost to get brokers to steer people to a particular mutual fund. For mutual funds that generally have low fees and no loads look to Vanguard or T. Rowe Price as they are some of the industry leaders in low-cost mutual funds that have a history of good performance.

Investing 101: A Basic Guide to Investing for Beginners by Kirk G. Meyer

While on the subject of brokers let us examine something while we are in this section. Not all brokers have your best interest in mind. In fact, most brokers are paid on how much and how often you buy and sell. Remember the mutual funds with loads? Brokers are the main people pushing these to investors as that is part of their compensation package. A broker has no legal obligation to keep your best interest in mind when advising you on what to buy and sell.

On the other hand, a Registered Investment Advisor, or RIA, has a legal obligation and a fiduciary trust responsibility to keep your best interests in mind when making recommendations. This is also where a fee-only financial advisor can come in handy as they are paid a set amount to do the work on your financial plans and portfolios that you agree upon. As a general rule, they are less expensive than an advisor that charges about 1% of all assets under management to do the same things. But that is not to say that a financial advisor who charges 1% of assets under management is a bad thing if they can outperform the markets and advise you on how to take advantages of tax laws to maximize your returns. All of these things need to be considered when choosing a partner in which you wish to work with.

I strongly advise reading the rest of this book and applying what you learn along with anything else you read on the subject as the more knowledge in this area the better off you will be. But as far as on-line brokers go here are a few things to remember. First, never pay more than $10 for a trade as many are about $6.95 and I have even seen a few as low as $2.95 a trade. But the ones on

Investing 101: A Basic Guide to Investing for Beginners by Kirk G. Meyer

the lower end may not meet the rest of the criteria I will set out. Second, it is important that you do not have to pay maintenance fees no matter what your balance is. Most on-line brokerage firms charge no fees, but it is always wise to read and fully understand the agreement before you start using them. Third, on-line quotes are a must when dealing with investments so make sure the brokerage firm is capable of those. And in conjunction with on-line quotes, it may be helpful to have on-line calculators to aid you in setting investment goals. And finally, and this is a personal one with me but may also be important to you as well, and that is the ability to buy fractional shares or reinvest dividends in fractional shares. Many brokerage firms will reinvest the dividends but will not allow you to buy in fractional shares. That is a handy feature when you invest a set amount on a regular basis and are doing dollar cost investing.

Investing 101: A Basic Guide to Investing for Beginners by Kirk G. Meyer

The Impact of Taxes

Depending on where you are keeping your investments the single largest factor that will work against you are the taxes associated with each. When it comes to where to place your investments you have three basic choices available to you. If you are employed, you may have a company sponsored 401(k) plan in which to invest which is a tax-advantaged account. Depending on your income you may have an Individual Retirement Account or IRA available to you. Technically these accounts are available to everyone, but their tax advantages may be limited to those who earn less but regardless their assets grow in a tax-deferred environment just as in a 401(k) account. And finally, a normal brokerage account that is not tax advantaged in any way at all. In a brokerage account, the assets are taxed as they are bought and sold and if they have any dividends paid on them.

Now that you know you will be placing your money in assets in one of these three accounts it is time to look at how they will be taxed and when. First, let us look at the four types of taxes we will be paying on our investments. The main tax people are concerned with is the ordinary income tax which is placed on all income earned and withdrawals of funds from 401(k) accounts and IRA's at age 59 ½. These taxes can be fairly low in instances where you do not earn very much or for high-income earners, as high as 39.6% on some of your income in 2016. Next are capital gains taxes which used to be fairly straightforward and simple but since 2012 that is not necessarily the case. Capital gains taxes are broken down into two categories, short-term and long-term. Short-term capital gains are on investments that are held less than a year and sold for a profit. These capital gains are taxed at your ordinary income tax rate and can be as high as 39.6%. Long-term capital gains are a bit more complicated as there are different rates involved. Regardless these are gains on the sale of investments that were held longer than a year and are taxed accordingly. For those in the lowest two tax brackets, there is no long-term capital gains tax owed. For the majority of the taxpayers, the long-term capital gains rate is still 15%. But for the higher income tax brackets, the long-term rate is now 20% and no longer 15%. Dividends are another aspect of the new tax bill for 2012 that we see a difference. Similar to long-term capital gains dividends are split into three areas. The lowest two tax brackets there are no taxes owed on qualified dividends, then it is 15% for the majority and then 20% for the highest income tax brackets. Ordinary dividends are still taxed as ordinary income for tax purposes. And the fourth type of tax we see is state and local income taxes. As the Federal government is the only one, who separates the type and source of the income, state and local taxes are an ordinary income tax. Unless that is, you are lucky enough to live in one of the seven states that currently have no income tax imposed on its citizens.

Now that you have a basic understanding of the tax structure it is time to look at the vehicles in which you can use to invest in. First, we will examine the employer-sponsored 401(k) plans. Like any investment vehicle, there are positives and negatives of each. One of the main positives about 401(k) plans is most companies will

Investing 101: A Basic Guide to Investing for Beginners
by Kirk G. Meyer

use a matching program as an incentive to get employees to contribute. I work for the Federal government, and while we do not have a 401(k), we do have the Thrift Savings Plan which works in the same fashion. The government like many private companies will match employee contributions up to a point. In my plan they will match every 5% I contribute with 4% meaning I get an automatic return on my funds. So always contribute up to the point where your company will match your contributions. Otherwise, you are leaving free money on the table. And that free money can make a huge difference when it comes to your retirement accounts. By taking advantage of my company match, I will basically double my savings power without considering anything else. Another advantage of contributing to your 401(k) account is it could lower your taxable income as some contributions are done on a pre-tax basis meaning they will lower your income by the amount you contribute. And all of these funds within the 401(k) grow tax deferred meaning you pay no taxes on the growth within the account. This means that more of your money will be working for you for many years to come. And another aspect of the 401(k) is that you are allowed to contribute up to $18,000 to these accounts in 2016 with an additional $6,000 for those over the age of 5o.

The negatives are far outweighed by the positives of the 401(k). One of the negatives is that the funds in these accounts are off limits to those who are not 59 ½ years old unless you are prepared to pay ordinary income tax on the withdrawal as well as a 10% early withdrawal penalty. These accounts are not considered to be liquid

Investing 101: A Basic Guide to Investing for Beginners
by Kirk G. Meyer

by nature and are meant to be seen as a long-term savings tool to help fund your retirement. And the second major negative is that all proceeds are taxed as ordinary income no matter what. If the investment were in a brokerage account, the proceeds could possibly be taxed at a more favorable long-term capital gains. But these two negatives are not reason enough to not contribute to a workplace 401(k).

Individual Retirement Accounts or as they are better known, IRA's are another option to save for retirement. They are similar to 401(k) plans but generally are done on an individual basis. The rules surrounding IRA's are also similar to 401(k) plans with there being a minimum age of 59 ½ to withdrawal funds. And like the 401(k), IRA's require mandatory withdrawals starting at age 70 ½ otherwise you will face stiff penalties. Unlike a 401(k) where you are allowed to contribute $18,000 for those under the age of 50, you are only allowed to contribute $5,500 or $6,500 for those over the age of 50. That is quite a difference between the two accounts, but that does not mean you can afford to ignore the IRA.

Now both 401(k) plans and IRA's have an option for ROTH accounts. While not every employer will offer a ROTH 401(k), it is an option at many locations. The ROTH IRA is available to those who qualify under the current IRS guidelines which change on a regular basis so always check to see that you are eligible to contribute to an IRA. So why would you pick a ROTH account? Well, for those in lower tax brackets now it makes good sense for the money you will take out in retirement will most likely be taxed at a higher rate. Also, it is a little easier to maximize

Investing 101: A Basic Guide to Investing for Beginners
by Kirk G. Meyer

your contributions as they are done on a pre-tax basis making it easier to reach the contribution levels of both IRA's and 401(k) plans.

There are some unique aspects of ROTH accounts that need to be discussed. In a 401(k) where you contribute to the plan your contributions are placed in a ROTH account as the funds, there have been taxed. As for the company match, those funds have not been taxed and are therefore placed in a Traditional account. In ROTH IRA's the principal may be withdrawn at any time unless it is a converted account in which there is a time frame in which the principal cannot be withdrawn. And ROTH accounts must be in place at least five years before the first withdrawal at age 59 ½ or a penalty will be imposed. And finally, ROTH IRA's do not have a minimum withdrawal starting at age 70 ½ for original owners.

If you do not qualify for a ROTH IRA due to the fact you earn too much there is a solution for you concerning this. What you need to do is open a non-deductible IRA and then do a conversion to a ROTH IRA. As the IRA was non-deductible in the first place, meaning the taxes were paid on the funds, no taxes will be due on the contribution when the IRA is converted to a ROTH account. The only taxes that will be due would be on any gains in the IRA from when the contributions happened, and the conversion to the ROTH IRA occurred.

So with these tax-advantaged accounts why someone would want to have a taxable brokerage account? Well, the answer is somewhat simple and can be complex at the same time. A brokerage account is the better place

Investing 101: A Basic Guide to Investing for Beginners by Kirk G. Meyer

to put money that you will need before you reach age 59 ½. Meaning you can invest and pay the taxes as you earn on these funds but have the liberty to access the funds for any reason at any age. This is a major advantage for people who may use a brokerage account for mid to long term savings goals that will be spent before age 59 ½. Another reason people use taxable brokerage accounts is that they have maximized their contributions to their 401(k) plan and IRA already. After you maximize these accounts, a brokerage account is about all that is left for you to save.

And there is another reason that it is important to have some of each of these accounts, the Traditional IRA or 401(k), a ROTH IRA or 401(k) and a taxable brokerage account. In retirement, it can be important to take funds from one account over another for tax purposes. And if you have some of each you will be able to possibly maximize your withdrawals to maximize your income while minimizing your income taxes. This is where it is a good idea to seek out a tax professional or financial planner.

Investing 101: A Basic Guide to Investing for Beginners by Kirk G. Meyer

Investment Plans

An investment plan is a plan in which you will outline how you will save and invest with the goal of retirement in mind. This is the frustrating part as no one really knows what it is that they will need in their retirement. But the plan should have an end game of retirement in mind when you develop one by yourself or with a financial planner.

For most, the first and most basic question we have about our retirement is how much will I need? In order to address this question in an adequate manner, you must first look at what you are doing now. Here if you budget that will make things easier and if not then it is time to start a budget. Without knowing where your money is going how will you ever know what you will need in retirement? First, you need to determine how much of your income you will need to replace once you do retire. Here you need to consider pensions, savings, and Social Security to come up with a figure that you will need in order to live. And then you will be able to figure out how much you can comfortably withdrawal from your savings to sustain your lifestyle. Once this is done, you can work backward to see how much you need to save in order to have the lifestyle you want in retirement.

So you have a budget of what you spend now, and you look for areas that will be cut or reduced in retirement. Then you will have an idea of what it is you will need to replace and save towards. Most people will have lower expenses in retirement, but that is not always the case. In some instances, people buy vacation homes or plan to

Investing 101: A Basic Guide to Investing for Beginners
by Kirk G. Meyer

travel the world more than they ever did while working. However, on average the typical person will need to have $2/3^{rds}$ of their income replaced in retirement.

So what do you do if your investment plan is not adequate? Consider working past the age of 62 or 65 until your full retirement age of 67. This will allow you to save more, get more of a pension if your company offers one and add to your Social Security benefits. The longer you can delay taking Social Security the more your benefits will be. And always consider all sources of income when developing what it is you need to save in your investment plan. Include pensions, IRA's 401(k)'s, and always Social Security. These are people's main sources of income in retirement, and all need to be considered when developing your investment plan.

So you have the portion of your income that you need to replace from your budget and basis of expenses in retirement. Add all of those items up and that is one portion of what your investment plan needs to address. Then figure what expenses you will incur that are not current expenses such as extra travel to see grandchildren. Or the purchase of a vacation home. Add that portion to your investment plan. Together these expenses will be the basis of what it is you will need to save.

Then you need to create a plan that will assist you in reaching your funding needs. So how long does a basic plan need to fund timewise? The answer to that is you need to figure on at least 25 years of retirement. And in your plan, you need to remember that your assets within your portfolio will continue to grow during that projected 25 years of retirement.

So now we have how much money we need to save and how long we will need the money to last. Next, we will figure out how much money you can withdrawal on an annual basis. Industry experts have for years said that under normal circumstances a person could safely withdrawal 4% from their retirement accounts without having to fear too much about running out of money. That is unless you are in retirement during a severe bear market meaning the markets are down considerably from where they need to be to protect your principal.

I believe that with more people leaving a larger portion of their retirement portfolios in equities to keep pace with inflation and longer life expectancies you may actually be able to take out a little larger percentage. If you assume you will at least make a 2% return after inflation you should be able to withdrawal 5% a year safely. As an example of what you need to save to have a $50,000 a year withdrawal, you would need to save a million dollars. Or 0.05 times $1,000,000 is a $50,000 annual payment towards your retirement income.

So we have all the pieces needed to develop our investment plan. So we take these pieces and use them to calculate our savings needs. But first, we need to make some assumptions that will enable us to reach our final objective. What do you think inflation will be? What do you expect your portfolio to return on an annual basis? And finally, how long or how many years do you have until you retire? Once you know these final items you

Investing 101: A Basic Guide to Investing for Beginners by Kirk G. Meyer

have everything that you need to develop an investment plan. But where do you invest? That is where you need to look at the three different locations in which people invest for retirement, the IRA, the 401(k) and a brokerage account.

For a basic investing plan the following is a good starting point for most people. First, if your employer offers a match on its 401(k), take full advantage of getting that free money. That means contribute at least as much as needed to take full advantage of the match. Then, if you have high-interest debts pay those down and try to avoid accumulating any additional debts that are not paid off on a monthly basis except possibly an auto loan, student loans, and mortgages on primary residences.

If you can do the first two steps, you are now in a position to establish the much needed and extremely important emergency fund. Ideally, you should save six months' worth of expenses if you do not have a stable or highly dependable source of income. In the event your job is considered stable you may be able to get by with three months' worth of expenses. However, I do recommend at least six months' worth to be on the safe side as nothing is guaranteed in today's world of finance. So what is considered high debt that needs to be paid down before the creation of an emergency fund? I say anything that is costing you over 8% or 10% is considered a high-interest debt that needs to be paid off before you begin saving your emergency fund. But I also recommend you always have at least a $1,000 saved for smaller emergencies that always seem to pop up as well.

Investing 101: A Basic Guide to Investing for Beginners by Kirk G. Meyer

Now you are saving up to the match in your 401(k) at work, have paid off high-interest debt and have established a fully funded emergency fund it is time to fund your IRA. If you are not eligible for an IRA, remember you can always contribute to a non-deductible IRA and convert it to a ROTH at any time. After your IRA is maxed out as well, it could be time to go back to funding your 401(k) at work if your plan offers good investment choices that are reasonable in price to maintain. Remember fees eat at your investments so keep those in mind as well when you think of going back to funding a 401(k). If you max out your contributions to your 401(k) or the investment choices are not such that you want to invest in the plan it will be time to invest in a brokerage account.

If you have children or have a family member attend college, remember to include college savings plans such as State sponsored 529 plans in your investment plan. These are important and must be considered in your plan as substantial amounts of funds can be accumulated in these accounts and they must be accounted for in any investment plan.

Returns and How to Consider Them

Now that you have your investment plan it is time to examine how you want to go about achieving your goals in regards to the returns on your portfolio. There are two basic trains of thought on this subject, and that is one of what I consider passive and active managed portfolios. And you can look at them in this light as well. Passively managed portfolios focus on the beta which is the exposure to the overall market risks. And actively managed portfolios tend to be geared towards the alpha which is the difference between your portfolio and the markets. Now this is a basic view of these two ways to look at your portfolio's returns, but this is as far as we need to go without getting into the heaving lifting of returns, which could be its own book.

So which should you focus on? In my opinion, you need always to focus on the beta returns as achieving the alpha returns on a consistent basis is nearly impossible. Even for the professional money managers as they will rarely beat the beta and the markets for a prolonged period of time. So how do you invest to take advantage of beta returns? In today's financial world this is becoming easy, through indexed mutual funds and exchange traded funds.

Find a good mutual fund or exchange traded fund that follows an index that you wish to have your portfolio matched to and buy the one that is with a reliable financial firm and has low management fees. Remember fees are your enemy here and matching the market returns is the name of the game as on average the

Investing 101: A Basic Guide to Investing for Beginners
by Kirk G. Meyer

market has returned about 9% since 1900. If you have a mutual fund that charges 1% management fee and inflation is 3%, which leaves an actual return of 5% on your investment. Now an indexed exchange traded fund, such as one from Vanguard, that is indexed to the S&P 500 could save you almost 0.9% over a mutual fund can be worth thousands over a 30 plus year period in a retirement account.

If you are after alpha returns in your portfolio, which I advise against, you are looking at the portfolio's return and marking it against that of the market. Now all investments carry risk, and no returns are guaranteed. But in alpha investing you are taking on more risks thereby creating a larger potential reward for your portfolio. But on the downside, the potential for larger losses is also present which is why I always recommend going for the beta returns.

Regarding significance, the beta is also more significant than alpha due to the overall exposure. In a beta return, the exposure is less significant than the exposure to the ups and downs of the overall market. One of the main reasons for this is by investing for the beta returns and using indexed funds you can diversify easily and can spread your exposure over many different sectors of the investing world. And by using different indexes, you can even further spread the diversification over different sectors but also different sized companies as well. Plus, you can get exposure to all sorts of different asset classes as well and investments from around the world. With six well-selected exchange traded funds you can achieve an extremely diversified portfolio that can reduce your market risks and increase potential returns.

On the other side if you are after alpha returns you are in an arena that is more geared towards actively managed portfolios. While in some instances actively managed portfolios do beat the markets it is extremely difficult to do this on a consistent long-term basis. And with actively managed portfolios comes additional management fees and trading costs. Which as discussed can eat into your portfolio's performance and your bottom line in the way of missed gains. And if you are considering managing your alpha portfolio think of this first, 97% of professionally managed funds fail to beat the beta return.

Let us examine how to get beta returns in a little more detail. Some people will use mutual funds because they have been around longer and more people are familiar with them as an investment tool. But there are drawbacks to using mutual funds. One they are bought and sold only once a day after the market has closed and the Net Asset Value or NAV has been calculated. Then there are the management fees, on average the typical mutual fund's fee is about 1.3% annually.

Now let us compare mutual funds to the newer exchange traded funds that are operated by many of the same financial institutions as, the older mutual funds. An exchange-traded fund, or ETF, is very similar to a mutual fund in that it tracks an index or follows so sort of investment strategy. Unlike mutual funds the exchange traded fund trades throughout the day the same as an

Investing 101: A Basic Guide to Investing for Beginners by Kirk G. Meyer

individual company's stock. And finally, there is the difference in fees. Some of the exchange traded funds that follow widely accepted indexes will charge an annual fee as low as 0.05%. Now that is a way to enhance your portfolio's long-term success if you saved over 1.2% annually on fees as compared to some mutual funds. Exchange-traded funds also do not tend to manage their portfolios in an active manner causing fewer trading fees and tax events such as capital gains. The last point is more applicable to mutual funds or exchange traded funds held in taxable brokerage accounts.

Some additional difference between the two investments is liquidity. In some of the smaller exchange traded funds you may need to wait for a buyer of the fund as it does trade like a stock under the supply and demand pricing strategy. All mutual funds can sell assets to create liquidity which is a reason why they have more taxable events than an exchange traded fund. And since exchange traded funds trade like stocks there are commission fees associated with purchasing and selling. But like many mutual funds, there are several discount brokerage firms and financial companies that offer free trades if you purchase through their platform. By using a firm that allows for free trades people are free to take advantage of dollar cost averaging investing. That is buy a dollar amount at set intervals no matter what the market is doing. When the markets are down you are simply buying more shares, and when they are up, you buy fewer. Over a long period, you will be ahead of people who tried to time the markets. But this approach

Investing 101: A Basic Guide to Investing for Beginners
by Kirk G. Meyer

only makes sense if the fees associated with the purchase are small or better yet, free.

Investing 101: A Basic Guide to Investing for Beginners by Kirk G. Meyer

Different Asset Classes

Different asset classes are the key to true diversification, not just owning a group of index mutual or exchange traded funds. And the reason for that is if you just own a group of funds you own a broad range of equities in different companies. In other words, a single asset class, equities. So what are some asset classes? Well, the most widely known and popular are stocks or equities that are traded on the secondary markets. But that is not all that there is by any means. There are different bonds, federal government issues, state or county issues or private company issued bonds. And these bonds all come with different risks. There is also real estate to consider. Be that by owning rental property yourself or by purchasing a grouping of different properties through the use of a real estate investment trust or as they are better known REIT's. And let us not forget that there are these same investments in the international markets and emerging markets as well. Want to own commodities such as silver and gold? There are exchange traded funds for those as well. So by having different funds in some of these different asset classes, you can achieve more diversification and further reduce your portfolio's risk. With some research into individual mutual funds or exchange traded funds you can easily own a wide variety of these and other different asset classes.

First, we will examine stocks or equities. This is the most widely held asset class that there is and for good reason. It has the potential to provide the greatest rewards in the form of returns. Stocks will make money for you in one of two ways, through the payment of dividends or if you

Investing 101: A Basic Guide to Investing for Beginners by Kirk G. Meyer

sell the stock for profit or capital gain. Most stocks in the US are sold in the secondary markets which as the New York Stock Exchange or NYSE or the NASDAQ which started as the first computer based stock exchange. In these and other regional exchanges throughout the US, stocks are bought and sold on a daily basis. US based equities are the preferred investment for many because of the regulatory environment, the strong accounting practices and sales are based on the US dollar reducing currency risks.

But the US is not the only country with an equity market system. Many international locations have their own versions of the NYSE where equities of that country are traded. And in today's financial world even emerging markets and under-developed countries have their own exchange markets. When someone invests in these markets, there are additional risks that most US equities do not have to face. Some are based on the political climate of that country, it currency valuation, different tax treatments, and the risk associated with developing countries in general.

For international countries, you should look to Europe, Japan, Australia and certain other Southeast Asian countries if you seek more stable returns and better regulation and accounting practices. Most of the safer international countries tend to fall into the capitalism format, have a strong sense of the rule of law, and a currency that is considered a major one and somewhat more stable than that of developing countries. Then there are emerging markets in some of the world's larger but less developed economies of the world. The most

Investing 101: A Basic Guide to Investing for Beginners
by Kirk G. Meyer

famous emerging markets make up the BRIC which stands for Brazil, Russia, India, and China. In these countries, there is a good chance for massive returns, but they are also subject to massive losses and are therefore considered riskier than an investment in a major international market. And finally, there are developing markets in many countries found in less developed locations such as the Middle East, Africa, and South America. In many instances, these developing countries will be upgraded and move up to emerging market status. These are some of the riskiest equity investments that there are so invest at your own risk.

Bonds are perhaps the second most owned asset class. Like stocks they come in all shapes, sizes and varieties. Bonds, unlike stocks, do not represent a piece of ownership in a company or government but rather are a sort of IOU. Bonds are purchased for face value, or a discount, and pay interest on a set schedule and then the principal when the bond matures. These financial instruments are considered a safer investment than stocks. A reason for this is that is a company declares bankruptcy a bond holder will always be paid before a holder of the company's stock. In the US the main types of bonds are Treasury, corporate, mortgage-backed securities, and municipal. Each is unique and has its own set of risks.

A Treasury is considered the safest of all bonds as they are issued by the Federal governments. These bonds are considered to be risk-free as the US has never defaulted on interest or principal payment. However, there is interest rate risk involved with Treasuries. That is

Investing 101: A Basic Guide to Investing for Beginners by Kirk G. Meyer

basically the chance that you invest in a bond, and interest rates change causing your bonds value to go up or down depending on which way the interest rate goes. Foreign countries also issue bonds but depending on the issuing country will determine the risks associated with the ownership of that bond.

Corporate bonds are the second safest bonds to own depending on the financial strength of the issuing company. Highly rated companies will pay a lower interest rate than those that are not as financially secure or rated lower. The more risk that there is that a payment may be missed equates to a higher interest rate that must be paid to investors to compensate for the additional risk. If you invest in a foreign company's bond, you will not only face the issues mentioned but also a currency exchange risk.

Mortgage back securities are bonds issued, at least in the US, by quasi-governmental entities such as Fannie Mae and Freddie Mac. These are bonds that are secured by pools of mortgages that are residences throughout the country. They are pooled and sold by the two mentioned companies as well as other large financial institutions. These bonds carry the risk of someone defaulting on their mortgage creating a loss for the bond as well as a prepayment risk. Meaning people pay off their loans faster than originally anticipated or they refinance due to lower interest rates.

The final bond we will examine is the municipal bond. These are bonds issued by states and counties for the building of roads, airports, and other infrastructure projects within their tax authority. These bonds are relatively safe and are tax advantaged in nature. In most instances, they are exempt from income tax and thereby pay a lower interest rate than most corporate bonds as the return is similar after all tax incentives are considered. People with higher net worth's tend to own municipals and not in tax advantaged accounts. And like all bonds, they carry interest rate risk depending on the way interest rates go over time.

Real Estate Investment Trusts or REIT's are a way to own a diversified portfolio of real estate. These are companies that own commercial properties and operate them for profit. Then by law, the company must pay out a majority of the company's profits in the form of dividends to shareholders. These assets perform well when the equity markets are down, and inflation is considered high, but not always. As with any investment, there are many factors that can influence the overall performance of the REIT in question. A reason REIT's can pay such handsome dividends is that the company pays no income tax and hence why the majority of the profits must be paid as dividends and the REIT's individual owners as they pay taxes on the dividends in their income tax returns.

And finally, though by no means the last asset class available, are commodities. Commodities can be precious metals such as gold and silver, lumber, oil and natural gas, grains or even livestock. Now it is not very practical to own commodities in the physical sense as many are bulky and would require large areas for storage. And while it is possible to own precious metals

Investing 101: A Basic Guide to Investing for Beginners by Kirk G. Meyer

they as a rule have been fairly poor investments in regards to their returns over a long period of time. But through exchange traded funds you can own any or all of the commodities mentioned as well as many others. Also, you can get exposure to commodities through companies that deal in them. Want exposure to gold but do not want to own actual gold? How about investing in a company that mines gold. Want exposure to oil? Consider oil exploration and refining companies such as Exon Mobile. By own companies involved in the production of the commodity you can have exposure to the commodity indirectly.

Investing 101: A Basic Guide to Investing for Beginners by Kirk G. Meyer

Diversification

When it comes to investing the most important decision that you can make is about your asset allocation and the diversification of your portfolio. With some research and the proper placement of assets, diversification can decrease the risk of your portfolio and increase the portfolio's returns. So you may be asking yourself why the previous section was so detailed? Well, the answer is fairly simple. You use the types of assets discussed in the previous section to diversify your own portfolio.

From the assets discussed and the others that were not that still exist, use a combination that you are comfortable with to reduce your portfolio's risk. As one asset goes down others will generally go up. That combination is what reduces the overall risk of your portfolio. And as a result of such a reduction of the portfolio's risk, you can achieve better overall returns than an all-equity portfolio. The reason for this is that a single asset class tends to move in the same direction regardless of their minor differences. This means that despite the fact equities have outperformed all other asset classes, one would think that owning nothing but a wide and diverse selection of equities would be the best route. Well, that works well when equities go up but as in 2008 and 2009 when they saw drops of nearly 50% a truly diversified portfolio would not have gone down nearly as much. And when a portfolio does not go down as much as one invested in nothing but equities it does not have as far to go to get back to even. Meaning a well-diversified portfolio can and does decrease the market risks associated with it but can also increase the portfolio's overall returns.

As I just alluded to in the previous paragraph. A portfolio is not considered diversified if you own anything but equities that are in different sectors or industries. While that can be of assistance in a real diversified portfolio of assets, it is not considered diversified. As a fast and easy to explain sample, let us examine a mock portfolio of six exchange-traded funds. One is a fund that tracks the S&P 500 to provide exposure to the largest 500 companies in the US. A second fund tracks nothing but small capitalized equities, meaning a market capitalization under $2 billion. Many times these equities will outperform larger blue chip stocks, and their movements are not always in the same direction. Then a third fund could be in emerging markets to provide exposure to foreign markets. As in many instances, a fund that is invested in emerging markets can and often does go in a different direction that the US markets. A fourth fund can be invested in REIT's to provide a countercyclical approach to equities as REIT's generally perform better when equities are down, and inflation is higher. Then the final two funds can be invested in US Treasury bonds with variable maturity dates and high-grade corporate bonds. So with just the use of six different exchange traded funds you cover four different asset classes and give your portfolio some real diversification in the process.

The type of portfolio just described is an easy one to replicate and is also designed to decrease its risk and increase its returns. Yes, three of the funds are in equities, and two are in bonds but the use described is a

Investing 101: A Basic Guide to Investing for Beginners
by Kirk G. Meyer

diversified one. The two funds that are invested in US equities are a large cross section of the 500 largest companies that are not concentrated in any one sector. And then the second is invested in almost 2,000 small companies that are even more diverse than the S&P 500. And of course, the third fund is in foreign emerging markets which have very little in common with the US equity funds. Both bond funds are counter-cyclical to the US equity funds and will go in the opposite direction from each other. And REIT's are a distinct fourth asset class that acts much the same way bonds do with equities, as opposites.

A distinct key to diversification is to have as many asset classes that you can manage. While more can be better, it still has to be an amount that is manageable. A better sample portfolio would include some extra asset classes and one in particular that has not been discussed before. If possible, it would be good to have not only small and large equities in the US in your portfolio but equities from established foreign markets in addition to emerging markets. Then, of course, you will still have the REIT and at least a single bond fund in the mixture. Then if you can add a fund that specializes in commodities of some form for some added diversification. And finally, the new asset class that has not been discussed but is one that can be a powerful asset to have in your portfolio and that is a Treasury Inflation Protected Security which will provide not only diversification to your portfolio but also some added protection in the event of high inflation. These are also known as TIPS.

Investing 101: A Basic Guide to Investing for Beginners by Kirk G. Meyer

One of the most successful investors not named Warren Buffett is the head of Yale's endowment. David Swensen recommends a portfolio that is made up of the following assets by percentage. 20% in US equities, 20% in REIT's, 15% in international equities, 5% emerging markets, 15% TIPS and 15% Treasuries. While I may not agree with 15% in Treasuries, you can always diversify the bonds by using different types and varieties. You can also decrease the bonds some and add an exchange-traded fund that invests in commodities.

As you get closer go retirement, you may want to shift your asset allocation some to become more conservative in nature. In the past, financial advisors would suggest a more bond heavy portfolio and reduce equities. As people live longer in retirement, there is a need to keep growing one's portfolio and not simply rely on income-producing bonds. What was used was take 100 then subtract your age and invest that figure in equities. Which means if you were 70 years old it would mean that 100-70 equals 30% invested in equities. I find that to me a little too conservative for today's needs. It can easily be stated that a portfolio that is 50% invested in equities but high-quality blue chip dividend paying equities can be better for the health of the portfolio than one that is 30% equities and 70% bonds.

Investing 101: A Basic Guide to Investing for Beginners by Kirk G. Meyer

General Thoughts

We have covered a fair amount of information up to this point, and now we will simply examine some tips and thoughts to end the book.

It is imperative that you have an investment plan and one that lays out a detailed plan for your asset allocation or your plan for diversification. An easy way to achieve this is through the use of exchange-traded funds. Two financial companies that have an excellent choice of exchange traded funds are Vanguard and iShares.

If a two or more similar mutual funds or exchange traded funds are equal in what they invest in, then it is time to look to what is the percentage of fees they charge and how liquid are they. In theory, a fund that is indexed to say the S&P 500 should perform the same as another so fees and liquidity can be a good determining factor.

As a rule, the larger mutual funds and exchange traded funds will have more assets under management. These larger funds are more liquid thereby meaning their spread between purchase and selling price will be smaller.

If you are interested in the Swensen model, there is an exchange-traded fund for each asset class. All you need to do is pick the best exchange traded fund for your needs and go with the one that fits best. What determines the best fit for you? That is going to be the fund with the lowest fees and the highest liquidity.

If you want to use dollar cost average investing you need to determine how much you will invest and select a discount broker to use. I like and have used Capital One Investing for over decade now and love its ease of use and features. Most brokers will make you buy your shares in whole shares, not Capital One if you use they automatic investment feature that costs only $4 a purchase and they will invest your whole amount and purchase fractional shares. They also will reinvest dividends for free as well and the best part they charge no maintenance fees.

A workplace 401(k) plan may not always have the best investment choices. Some plans use funds that charge extremely high management fees and others have a poor selection of funds, to begin with. Within your 401(k) plan look for a fund that has a broad exposure to the markets both for the US and International sectors. Try to find funds in the plan that follow a beta investing plan with regards to returns. Avoid sector based funds in your 401(k) as they are more geared towards alpha returns and as we have discussed the beta is the return you want to have in your portfolio. Also, fees in 401(k) plans tend to be on the higher side so look for funds with total fees around 1% of assets on an annual basis.

In all mutual funds, you want to seek out the best funds and the ones with the lowest fees just as you would in your 401(k) account. Also, seek out funds with high assets under management and those that have had their managers in place for several years. The manager is the one that will have been responsible for the fund's long-term track record, so that is a key aspect to consider as well. But remember, past performance is not an indication of the future performance by any means.

Investing 101: A Basic Guide to Investing for Beginners
by Kirk G. Meyer

So where do you keep what asset classes? That is a question that many do it yourself investors have, and there are some basic guidelines to follow. For REIT's and taxable bonds, the place you want to own them is in a retirement account where the higher taxed interest and dividends can grow tax-deferred for many years earning you, even more, money for retirement. If you are going to hold equities, exchange traded funds and mutual funds for the long-term it is okay to place them in either a taxable account based on the fact that long-term capital gains and dividends are taxed at a lower rate than most people's ordinary income. But they are also well served in tax-advantaged retirement accounts. I have some in each as I feel you need a mixture of taxable and tax advantaged accounts to properly prepare for retirement.

As for the TIPS that were mentioned in the diversification sections as an asset class, they are unique in nature. These are best kept in a retirement account due to the way that they are paid out. These investment vehicles are taxed as they earn interest and gain in value due to the inflation protection. And as these occur the owner is expected to pay taxes on income they have yet to receive. These realized as well as unrealized gains are both taxable in the year in which the gain occurred not when the bond matures.

Here is where most people make mistakes in the management of their portfolios. The key to investing is to buy when prices are low and sell when they are high. In a perfect world, this would be how everyone does this. However, most people do just the opposite as they buy

Investing 101: A Basic Guide to Investing for Beginners by Kirk G. Meyer

when prices are high and sell when everyone is in a panic at the lower prices. That is just human nature it seems and the way most of the investors act. Stay the course of your plans and remove the emotion from your investing.

If possible in your investment plan and asset allocation plan have exchange traded funds in the portfolio and not individual stocks. Individual stocks are riskier than an exchange traded fund and do not provide the level of diversification that funds provide.

As you have followed the advice in this book and had an asset allocation plan, you need to adhere to it at all times. It may change slightly from year to year as you approach retirement, but the changes should not be major in nature. And a key to maintaining a working asset allocation plan is to rebalance on a regular basis as well. Most of the time I recommend you rebalance when you review your plans at the end or beginning of the year.

Now I am not against the ownership of individual stocks, but that is something that requires a great deal of research and commitment to do successfully. You need to keep on top of what a company is doing and how they are performing. A portfolio that is well managed and diversified can afford to own 5% to 15% of the portfolio's value in stocks. It is always okay to play some as long as it is provided for in your plans. The key here is always to have your plan and its goals in mind when you invest in individual equities. You can use your IRA for these individual stocks and trade and invest in them within that investment vehicle. But try not to let your play funds become greater than 15% of your portfolio's total value.

Investing 101: A Basic Guide to Investing for Beginners by Kirk G. Meyer

Conclusion

As discussed throughout this book you can now see that investing does not have to be limited to the rich or those with financial advisors. Anyone with a little hard work and research can achieve a diversified portfolio that can help them withstand most economic conditions. Now I am not saying that under any circumstance will you never experience loss because we all do at some point. But by having the basics as provided in this book and the willingness to manage your own funds, you will be well on the way to a successful retirement.

Wealth creation is something anyone can do. There are even firms that will invest as little as $5 for you and charge only $1 a month to manage your diversified portfolio. One such site is www.acorns.com which takes a unique approach to investing the few cents you spend on a daily basis through what they call round ups. Then when you reach $5 they invest them in six exchange-traded funds. Sites like www.wealthfront.com and www.betterment.com take this approach and use a larger investing model to provide robo-advising much the same as Acorns. All these sites charge a small monthly fee to manage and diversify your portfolio including rebalancing the assets when they get too far out of balance.

Develop your plans and find what works for you then follow them to the best of your ability. Do not think that you cannot invest without the help of a professional. But if you do need one find a good fee-only financial planner to work with on an as needed basis.

Investing 101: A Basic Guide to Investing for Beginners
by Kirk G. Meyer

Now go forth and begin your investing life and create the wealth you deserve.

Investing 101: A Basic Guide to Investing for Beginners by Kirk G. Meyer

Thank You for Your Purchase

Thank you for purchasing this book, and I hope you found it useful in your journey to financial freedom. Please leave me a comment if you liked the book on Amazon at http://amzn.to/2cOTl9T.

If there is anything that you think I can improve on, please feel free to contact me and let me know and I will take all comments into consideration for future revisions of the book. You can find my contact information in the following section.

Investing 101: A Basic Guide to Investing for Beginners
by Kirk G. Meyer

About Kirk G. Meyer

Kirk G. Meyer's educational and work background is fairly diverse. He holds a BS in Business Administration from Haskell Indian Nations University in Lawrence, Kansas and an MBA and MS in Accounting from Strayer University in Washington, DC. He just finished the final course in an MS in Financial Planning from Bentley University in suburban Boston, Massachusetts. Mr. Meyer works for the federal government in the area of contracts and before his current position was a bank examiner for a federal regulatory agency. In addition to his education and work experience, he is also a registered independent life insurance agent in his home state of Tennessee, selling various life insurance and annuities to individuals and families in need of these types of products. His educational background and love of helping others make him an asset to those looking for assistance and guidance in financial and personal financial matters.

Investing 101: A Basic Guide to Investing for Beginners by Kirk G. Meyer

How to Contact Kirk G. Meyer

Feel free to email Kirk at kirk@kirkgmeyer.com.

Please follow Kirk's blog at www.kirkgmeyer.com and he welcomes any comments or suggestions on how to make his blog or eBooks better for you.

You can also follow Kirk on Twitter at @kirkgmeyer

You can follow Kirk on Facebook at www.facebook.com/kirkgmeyer

You can follow Kirk on LinkedIn at www.linkedin.com/in/kirkgmeyer

For a complete listing of Kirk's books, please visit his Amazon Author Page at Kirk G Meyer.

One Last Chance for the Free Gifts!

Again, as a big thank you for getting Investing 101, I want to offer you some valuable free gifts and a chance to get some on-going financial advice. Just for getting this book it entitles you to my Budget Spreadsheet and Debt Reduction Spreadsheet that I normally sell for a total of $10. It is yours free for getting Basics of Personal Finance and signing up for my free email newsletters that have previews to my ebooks, special articles that are geared towards personal finance and now access to these two valuable spreadsheets. To get your spreadsheets now simply go to my blogs website and sign up today. Visit www.kirkgmeyer.com today to get your free valuable spreadsheets.

Investing 101: A Basic Guide to Investing for Beginners by Kirk G. Meyer

Other Books by Kirk G. Meyer

Thrift Savings Plan: A Practical Guide to the TSP

The Basics of Life Insurance

A Brief Overview of Annuities

Financial Plans: Just the Basics

Personal Finance: A Grouping of Financial Topics

Final Expense Insurance

Budgeting 101

The Basics of Life Insurance and Annuities Bundle

Your Credit Report and You

The Basics of Personal Finance

www.ingramcontent.com/pod-product-compliance
Lightning Source LLC
Chambersburg PA
CBHW070409190526
45169CB00003B/1180

www.ingramcontent.com/pod-product-compliance
Lightning Source LLC
Chambersburg PA
CBHW070409190526
45169CB00003B/1180